Come unto me, all ye that labour and are heavy laden, and I will give you rest.

Matt. 11:28

LITTLE TALK
WITH THE
LORD

MARIE ANTOINETTE JEAN PIERRE

PRIMIX
PUBLISHING
THE WRITE CHOICE

Primix Publishing
East Brunswick Office Evolution
1 Tower Center Boulevard, Ste 1510
East Brunswick, NJ 08816
www.primixpublishing.com
Phone: 1-800-538-5788

Published by Primix Publishing: 11/27/2024

ISBN: 979-8-89194-294-3(sc)
ISBN: 979-8-89194-295-0(e)

Library of Congress Control Number: 2024916424

CONTENTS

PART VII

You must always love one another as brethren living together in Christ.

FOREWORD

Emmanuel Asser Jean-Pierre
Pastor
Marie Antoinette's uncle

He who wants to contemplate or personally have the experience of a profound inspiration by the Lord, will take the task of reading very carefully this little but wonderful art work *Little Talk with the Lord* of Marie Antoinette Jean-Pierre.

Marie Antoinette, a niece whom I admire, was born to Jérémy Jean-Pierre, my elder brother and his wife, Agnèce, whose maiden name was Guerrier. She has five brothers: Jocelyn, André, Rosemar, Charlemagne, Joseph; and three sisters: Jocelyne, Mamouse, and Raymonde.

I say all this to affirm that I perfectly know the author of the book for having seen her born and bloom. Antoinette is one of the most beautiful pearls of the Jean-Pierre family. That is the reason why her friends, classmates, and colleagues call her "Biblo" (beauty) and her close relatives call her "Nenette." She has always been a coddled child and interested in religion. But for a long time it seems that she has found her true eager soul desire: *Jesus of Nazareth*. The experience of Marie Antoinette recalls that of Marie at the feet of the Savior at Bethany. She prays, sings, preaches; she is attached to her church, and she writes in order to share her spiritual joys with all who desire establishing this intimate and constant relation with the Lord as well.

Dear readers, I invite you to read with interest *Little Talk with the Lord* lingering especially on these chapters: "Talking with the Lord," "Seven Keys of Deliverance," "The Psalms," "I Know My Savior," Good Morning Lord," "Jesus Will Never Change," "Victory," etc. Thus, you will discover how much the decision of the author to stay hidden under the wings of Jesus is firm, and determined; how the power of the Holy Spirit has inspired and fortified her, and how, animated by the same Spirit and influenced by the same divine strength, you will have the same experience: *living an authentic Christian life through Jesus.*

TALK WITH THE LORD

The Holy Book, the Bible gives
a considerable number of verses
demonstrating that God answers
the prayers of humans.

Undoubtedly, there are conditions in which one lives that blocks the blessings or the answer of God to our requests or prayers. For example, if one lives in sin without a sincere repentance, the favor of God will not be bestowed. But it is he who says in his word that if anyone has sinned, he has a lawyer by the Father, Jesus Christ the righteous one who intercedes for the forgiveness of our sins.

> *You shall seek me, and you shall find me if you seek me with all your heart.*
>
> Mark 11:24

Therefore I say unto you, What things soever ye desire, when ye pray, believe that ye receive them, and ye shall have them.

PART I

SEVEN KEYS FOR DELIVERANCE

Advices to follow for the success of this personal experience with God:

1. Avoid television, radio, etc.
2. Avoid all discussions even biblical ones.
3. Take a light nutrition.
4. Have a time to pray.
5. Be completely one with God.
6. Avoid stupid calls.
7. Drink a sufficient quantity of water.
8. Avoid all erotic relations.
9. Respect the precious hours of prayer.
10. 6:00 a.m.–9:00 a.m., 12:00 p.m.–3:00 p.m., and 6:00 p.m.
11. Choose your favorite songs.
12. Each day has its theme.

For example, first day—confession during the whole day.

FIRST DAY—FIRST KEY

General confessions

Read Ps. 51; Ps. 102; Ps. 143

In Ephesians 2:3, Paul says that we are by nature children of wrath. And David, in turn, in Psalm 58:4, "The wicked are estranged from the womb: they go astray as soon as they be born, speaking lies." In Romans 3:10, Paul says, "There is no righteous, not even one."

There arises the necessity of a sincere confession before starting a spiritual endeavor.

The known sin that cannot be forgiven, is the one for which we do not repent and do not ask for forgiveness. And here is an excellent example, the woman caught in adultery is sure to have gone too far. The head bowed down, the eyes facing the floor, she was waiting silently that the stones be beaten against her.
She was greatly surprised to discover that the door of grace was open to her.
She was not condemned. God offered to her once more his forgiveness and his strength. For the wages of sin is death, but the gift of God is eternal life through Jesus Christ our Lord.

SECOND DAY—SECOND KEY

Lay your plans at his feet
Read Ps. 42; Ps. 69; Ps. 139

Every human being, no matter his race, his color, his intellectual level, has some trouble: physical or moral sufferings that push him often to seek the Lord. In this case, it is important to do the inventory of your bad actions and say it all to the Lord. We must pray. You must pray until we are sure that you have said it all to the Lord. To be on the safe side, it is preferable to make a list. Do not be in a rush. Take time to talk to the Lord.

Share the most intimate secrets with him. And through this practice, you will see what God can do for his children in such a time as this.

THIRD DAY—THIRD KEY

Assurance

Read Ps. 46; Ps. 91; Ps. 27

The love of God reveals itself in our acting toward his people. We must discern with a clear and lucid view, in adversity as well as in sickness, in countertime as well as in trial, the light of the divine glory which reflects on the face of Christ and then trust in the rescuing hand of God, but we offend the Lord too often with our unbelief.

It is because we do not believe that we are forgiven that we continue to sin. Doubt leads to defeat; certainty leads to victory.

Assurance is based on three axes:
1-past
2-present
3-future

Past—". . . Christ died for our sins according to the scriptures . . ." (1 Cor. 15:3)

> Therefore being justified by faith, we have peace with God through our Lord Jesus Christ (Rom. 5:1)
> See also Ephesians 2:8.

Present—"Being confident of this very thing, that he which hath begun a good work in you will perform *it* until the day of Jesus Christ. (Phil. 1:6)

Future—For the which cause I also suffer these things: nevertheless I am not ashamed; for I know whom I have believed, and am persuaded that he is able to keep that which I have committed unto him against that day. (2 Tim. 1:6)

> And now, little children, abide in him; that, when he shall appear, we may have confidence, and not be ashamed before him at his coming. (1 John 2:28, Gal. 5:5)

FOURTH DAY—FOURTH KEY

Remember the miracles of the Lord.
Read Exod. 14; Exod. 15 and 16

1. Moses before the Red Sea
2. The experience of manna in the wilderness
3. The experience of the water of Mara
4. The wedding feast of Cana
5. The widow of Serepta
6. The resurrection of the daughter of Jarius
7. The healing of the centurion's servant

Through these accomplished miracles, we have the confidence that you are in good hands. Your hand in the hand of the Lord will allow you to enjoy his benefits.

FIFTH DAY—FIFTH KEY

Ask with faith
Read Heb. 11

> The apostle James says: he who doubts is like a wave
> of the sea driven with the wind and tossed. (James 1:6)

Have a manifested faith, a faith that gets hold of the invisible, an unshakable faith. Such a faith will assure to our souls the blessing of heaven. The heavier the darkness that encompasses you, the brighter must shine the light of faith and the Christian example. Our faith must cause us to penetrate through the other side of the veil, in the place where Jesus has entered for us.

NOTES

In the beginning, God created the heavens and the earth.

SIXTH DAY—SIXTH KEY

Believe that everything is possible.

The righteous have always obtained help from above. Some many times the enemies of God have gathered their strength and their science to destroy the character and the influence of humble Christians who have trusted in God. Men will separate themselves from their idols and of the world, and the world will not separate them from God. Christ, our present and all-powerful Savior, in him dwells all fullness. Christians must know that Christ is really a present truth for them.

SEVENTH DAY—SEVENTH KEY

Victory

Read Ps. 46; Ps. 118; Ps. 113; Ps. 150

The Christian life is both a walk and a struggle; but it is not the human power that can cause us to be victorious. It is in the area of the heart that the struggle has taken place, the greatest ever that the human being has been engaged in, and that has as objective personal submission to the will of God and to the sovereignty of his love. We must thank God for what he has done for us. For true victory consists in overcoming the habit of making efforts to be victorious.

PART II

LOVE

Cor.

13

Love

1 Though I speak with the tongues of men and of angels, and have not charity, I am become *as* sounding brass, or a tinkling cymbal.

2 And though I have *the gift of* prophecy, and understand all mysteries, and all knowledge; and though I have all faith, so that I could remove mountains, (Matt. 17:20; 21:21) · (Mark 11:23) and have not charity, I am nothing.

3 And though I bestow all my goods to feed *the poor,* and though I give my body to be burned, and have not charity, it profiteth me nothing.

4 Charity suffereth long, *and* is kind; charity envieth not; charity vaunteth not itself, is not puffed up,

5 doth not behave itself unseemly, seeketh not her own, is not easily provoked, thinketh no evil;

6 rejoiceth not in iniquity, but rejoiceth in the truth;

7 beareth all things, believeth all things, hopeth all things, endureth all things.

8 Charity never faileth: but whether *there be* prophecies, they shall fail; whether *there be* tongues, they shall cease; whether *there be* knowledge, it shall vanish away.

9 For we know in part, and we prophesy in part.

10 But when that which is perfect is come, then that which is in part shall be done away.

11 When I was a child, I spake as a child, I understood as a child, I thought as a child: but when I became a man, I put away childish things.

12 For now we see through a glass, darkly, but then face to face: now I know in part; but then shall I know even as also I am known.

13 And now abideth faith, hope, charity, these three; but the greatest of these *is* charity.

JESUS'S TEACHING ON PRAYER

Matt. 6:5–13

Luke 11:2–4

5   And when thou prayest, thou shalt not be as the hypocrites *are:* for they love to pray standing in the synagogues and in the corners of the streets, that they may be seen of men. (Luke 18:10–14) Verily I say unto you, They have their reward.

6   But thou, when thou prayest, enter into thy closet, and when thou hast shut thy door, pray to thy Father which is in secret; and thy Father which seeth in secret shall reward thee openly.

7   But when ye pray, use not vain repetitions, as the heathen *do:* for they think that they shall be heard for their much speaking.

8   Be not ye therefore like unto them: for your Father knoweth what things ye have need of, before ye ask him.

9   After this manner therefore pray ye:
    Our Father which art in heaven,
    Hallowed be thy name.

10   Thy kingdom come.
    Thy will be done
    in earth, as *it is* in heaven.

11   Give us this day our daily bread.

12   And forgive us our debts,
    as we forgive our debtors.

13   And lead us not into temptation,
    but deliver us from evil:
    For thine is the kingdom, and the power, and the glory, (1 Chron. 29:11) for ever. Amen.

I KNOW MY SAVIOR

He is the Alpha and Omega
He was born in Bethlehem

He is divine.
He forgives sins.
He heals the sick.
He resurrects the dead.
He lifts up the needy.
He restores the soul.
He is my god.
He is my lawyer.
He is my reference.
He is alive.
He intercedes for me.
He is my mediator.
He understands me.
He is always with me.

His name is *Jesus*.

THE CHURCH AND ITS TRUE NEEDS

The church needs more fraternity
The church needs more harmony
The church needs more unity
The church needs more peace
The church needs more sincerity
The church needs more understanding
The church needs more courtesy
The church needs more determination
The church needs more collaboration
The church needs more getting along
The church needs more togetherness
The church needs more devotion
The church needs more vigilance
The church needs more sincere souls.

Brothers, sisters, let us be united to accomplish our mission which is none other than saving souls.

DON'T EVER GIVE UP

You fell several times, but you may not remember
You fell a first time, you tried to stand back up.
You almost drowned a first time
You tried to swim.
You could miss the ball at first
Even the strongest
At times misses the ball
You could fall in the first exam.
Don't give up

When it seems to go wrong, instead of weeping, sing
Because singing is praying twice
Do not allow your tears to keep you from being
victorious
In the lion's dens you can triumph
In the midst of the fire you can triumph
No matter what trouble you are going through in
your life.
Don't give up.
Always believe you can start over with Jesus.

Biblo 2002

PART III

THE PATH IS FURTHER AHEAD.
CONTINUE WALKING.

TEN COMMANDMENTS

1. Precious Lord
2. Whose Crystal Palace
3. Pass Me Not
4. What a Friend
5. I Would Like to Tell You   **SING WITH ME**
6. Lord, Sanctify
7. I Was Drowning
8. The Love of God
9. For You
10. Lord, I Don't Have

Speaking to yourselves in psalms and hymns and spiritual songs, singing and making melody in your heart to the Lord . . .

Eph. 5:19

Precious Lord

Precious Lord, take my hand,
Lead me on, let me stand,
I am tired, I am weak, I am worn;
Through the storm, through the night,
Lead me on to the light:

Refrain

Take my hand, precious Lord,
Lead me home.

When my way grows drear,
Precious Lord, linger near,
When my life is almost gone,
Hear my cry, hear my call,
Hold my hand lest I fall:

Refrain

When the darkness appears
And the night draws near,
And the day is past and gone,
At the river I stand,
Guide my feet, hold my hand:

Refrain

Pass Me Not

Pass me not, O gentle Savior,
Hear my humble cry;
While on others Thou art calling,
Do not pass me by.

Refrain

Savior, Savior,
Hear my humble cry;
While on others Thou art calling,
Do not pass me by.

Let me at Thy throne of mercy
Find a sweet relief,
Kneeling there in deep contrition;
Help my unbelief.

Refrain

Trusting only in Thy merit,
Would I seek Thy face;
Heal my wounded, broken spirit,
Save me by Thy grace.

Refrain

Thou the Spring of all my comfort,
More than life to me,
Whom have I on earth beside Thee?
Whom in Heav'n but Thee?

Refrain

What a Friend We Have in Jesus

What a Friend we have in Jesus, all our sins and grief to bear!
What a privilege to carry everything to God in prayer!
O what peace we often forfeit, O what needless pain we bear,
All because we do not carry everything to God in prayer.

Have we trials and temptations? Is there trouble anywhere?
We should never be discouraged; take it to the Lord in prayer.
Can we find a friend so faithful who will all our sorrows share?
Jesus knows our every weakness; take it to the Lord in prayer.

Are we weak and heavy laden, cumbered with a load of care?
Precious Savior, still our refuge, take it to the Lord in prayer.
Do your friends despise, forsake you? Take it to the Lord in prayer!
In His arms He'll take and shield you; you will find a solace there.

Blessed Savior, Thou hast promised Thou wilt all our burdens bear
May we ever, Lord, be bringing all to Thee in earnest prayer.
Soon in glory bright unclouded there will be no need for prayer
Rapture, praise, and endless worship will be our sweet portion there.

No One Ever Cared for Me Like Jesus

CHORUS
No one ever cared for me like Jesus;
There's no other friend so kind as He;
No one else could take the sin and darkness from me.
O how much He cared for me!

I would love to tell you what I think of Jesus
Since I found in Him a friend so strong and true;
I would tell you how He changed my life completely,
He did something that no other friend could do.

CHORUS
No one ever cared for me like Jesus;
There's no other friend so kind as He;
No one else could take the sin and darkness from me.
O how much He cared for me!

All my life was full of sin when Jesus found me;
All my heart was full of misery and woe;
Jesus placed His strong and loving arms around me,
And He led me in the way I ought to go.

CHORUS
No one ever cared for me like Jesus;
There's no other friend so kind as He;
No one else could take the sin and darkness from me.
O how much He cared for me!

Ev'ry day He comes to me with new assurance,
More and more I understand His words of love;
But I'll never know just why He came to save me,
Till some day I see His blessed face above.

CHORUS

No one ever cared for me like Jesus;
There's no other friend so kind as He;
No one else could take the sin and darkness from me.
O how much He cared for me!

Love Lifted Me

I was sinking deep in sin, far from the peaceful shore,
Very deeply stained within, sinking to rise no more,
But the Master of the sea, heard my despairing cry,
From the waters lifted me, now safe am I.
Refrain: Repeat twice
Love lifted me! Love lifted me!
When nothing else could help
Love lifted me!
All my heart to Him I give, ever to Him I'll cling
In His blessed presence live, ever His praises sing,
Love so mighty and so true, merits my soul's best songs,
Faithful, loving service too, to Him belongs.
Refrain
Souls in danger look above, Jesus completely saves,
He will lift you by His love, out of the angry waves.
He's the Master of the sea, billows His will obey,
He your Saviour wants to be, be saved today.
Refrain

The Love of God

Her Royal Majesty,
QUEEN MARIE ANTOINETTE JEAN PIERRE THELIGENE
First Haitian-American African Queen
(Bmazazhi of Karu Kingdom in Africa)

The love of God is greater far
Than tongue or pen can ever tell;
It goes beyond the highest star,
And reaches to the lowest hell;
The guilty pair, bowed down with care,
God gave His Son to win;
His erring child He reconciled,
And pardoned from his sin.

Refrain:
Oh, love of God, how rich and pure!
How measureless and strong!
It shall forevermore endure—
The saints' and angels' song.
2. When hoary time shall pass away,
And earthly thrones and kingdoms fall,
When men who here refuse to pray,
On rocks and hills and mountains call,
God's love so sure, shall still endure,
All measureless and strong;
Redeeming grace to Adam's race—
The saints' and angels' song.
3. Could we with ink the ocean fill,
And were the skies of parchment made,
Were every stalk on earth a quill,
And every man a scribe by trade;
To write the love of God above
Would drain the ocean dry;
Nor could the scroll contain the whole,
Though stretched from sky to sky.

PART IV

Her Royal Majesty, Queen Bmazazhi Karu

When someone says they trust in God, it means they are certain that they will receive what they are waiting for. They have the conviction that the things we cannot see with our eyes exist for real.

WHEN I WAS IN TROUBLE

When I was in trouble, I called upon the Lord,
He answered me.
Deliver me, Lord from those who are lying.

PRAISE TO THE LORD

It is very good to sing to the Lord!
It is very good to sing to the Lord!
Yes, He is really worthy of it!
The Lord will rebuild the city of Jerusalem.
He will cause those of Israel who were scattered
in the midst of the other nations to return home.
He will give courage to those who mourn.
He will heal those who are hurt.
Our Lord is powerful. He is mighty.

COME AND DELIVER ME

Look in what misery I am.
Deliver me
Because I never forget your laws!
Defend my case.
Deliver me
Cause me to live again
As you have promised.

THE TRUE TOOL OF THE CHRISTIAN: PRAYER

Our God is approachable. He is understandable.
It is through prayer that human beings go to God and
God enters in human beings. One must pray without ceasing.
It is absurd to pray in the morning and to behave as a barbarian
during the rest of the day.
Some very short thoughts and mental invocations can keep the human
being in the presence of God.
Our whole behavior must be inspired by prayer. Prayer is as real
a force as universal gravity. Prayer is always followed by a result.
Prayer has an influence on both the spirit and the body. Prayer is
an elevation of the soul. Prayer is a conversation with God.

THE EFFECTS OF PRAYER

It can open the prison's doors.
It can heal the sick.
It can resurrect the dead.
It can fortify the downcast Christian.
It can change the will of God.
It can break the chains.
It can move mountains.
It can bring joy.
It can bring peace.
It can bring trust.

It brings triumph.
It is the master key.
It is our only safeguard.
More prayer, more power
More prayer, more grace
More prayer, more love
More prayer, more answer.

There is therefore now no condemnation
to them which are in Christ Jesus.

Integral Parts of a Christian Testimony:

1. The kingdom of God. Matthew 10:7; Luke 9:60; Acts 8:12
2. Repentance. Mark 1:4; Matthew 6:12
3. Deliverance. Luke 4:18, 19
4. Jesus Christ. Acts 5:42
5. Conversion. Acts 14:15
6. The word of faith. Romans 10:8
7. The Cross. 1 Corinthians 1:18
8. Christ crucified. 1 Corinthians 1:23
9. The denial of self. 2 Corinthians 4:5
10. The remission of sin. Luke 24:47 (Jerusalem)
11. Resurrection. Acts 4:2; 17; 18; 1 Corinthians 4:5
12. The forgiveness of sins. Acts 13:38
13. Peace. Ephesians 2:17
14. Righteousness. 2 Peter 2:5
15. The Gospel. Mark 1:14; Luke 9:6

To become a witness of Christ, the first step to take consists of living a personal experience with Him. It is not sufficient to have noticed a change in the life of others, or to have felt the power and the attraction of the gospel. The Christian testimony must always be founded on what one has lived. Not one soul will be impressed by a witness of Christianity who limits themselves saying, "I have perceived a great tumult, but I did not know what it was."

PART V

THE
PSALMS

PSALM FOR ASKING FORGIVENESS

Psalm 51
A Prayer for Cleansing
To the chief Musician, A Psalm of David, when
Nathan the prophet came unto him, <u>2.1</u>–<u>0.1</u>; <u>0.12</u>;
<u>15.15</u> after he had gone in to Bath-she'ba.

1   Have mercy upon me, O God,
according to thy loving-kindness:
according unto the multitude of thy tender mercies
blot out my transgressions.

2   Wash me thoroughly from mine iniquity,
and cleanse me from my sin.

3   For I acknowledge my transgressions:
and my sin *is* ever before me.

4   Against thee, thee only, have I sinned,
and done *this* evil in thy sight:
that thou mightest be justified when thou speakest,
and be clear when thou judgest. (Rom. 3:4)

5   Behold, I was shapen in iniquity;
and in sin did my mother conceive me.

6   Behold, thou desirest truth in the inward parts:
and in the hidden *part* thou shalt make me to know wisdom.

7   Purge me with hyssop, and I shall be clean:
wash me, and I shall be whiter than snow.

8   Make me to hear joy and gladness;
that the bones *which* thou hast broken may rejoice.

9   Hide thy face from my sins,
    and blot out all mine iniquities.
10   Create in me a clean heart, O God;
    and renew a right spirit within me.
11   Cast me not away from thy presence;
    and take not thy Holy Spirit from me.
12   Restore unto me the joy of thy salvation;
    and uphold me *with thy* free Spirit.
13   *Then* will I teach transgressors thy ways;
    and sinners shall be converted unto thee.
14   Deliver me from bloodguiltiness, O God,
    thou God of my salvation:
    and my tongue shall sing aloud of thy righteousness.
15   O Lord, open thou my lips;
    and my mouth shall show forth thy praise.
16   For thou desirest not sacrifice;
    else would I give *it:*
    thou delightest not in burnt offering.
17   The sacrifices of God *are* a broken spirit:
    a broken and a contrite heart, O God,
    thou wilt not despise.
18   Do good in thy good pleasure unto Zion:
    build thou the walls of Jerusalem.
19   Then shalt thou be pleased with the sacrifices of righteousness,
    with burnt offering and whole burnt offering:
    then shall they offer bullocks upon thine altar.

PSALM FOR TRUST

Psalm 4
An Evening Prayer of Trust in God
To the chief Musician on Neg'inoth,
A Psalm of David

1   Hear me when I call,
     O God of my righteousness:
     thou hast enlarged me *when I was* in distress;
     have mercy upon me, and hear my prayer.

2   O ye sons of men,
     how long *will ye turn* my glory into shame?
     How long will ye love vanity,
     and seek after leasing?

                                        Selah.

3   But know that the LORD hath set apart him that is godly
for himself:
     the LORD will hear when I call unto him.

4   Stand in awe, and sin not: (Eph. 4.26)
     commune with your own heart upon your bed, and be still.

                                        Selah.

5   Offer the sacrifices of righteousness,
     and put your trust in the LORD.

6   *There be* many that say, Who will show us *any* good?
     LORD, lift thou up the light of thy countenance upon us.

7   Thou hast put gladness in my heart,
      more than in the time *that* their corn and their wine
      increased.

8   I will both lay me down in peace, and sleep:
      for thou, LORD, only makest me dwell in safety.

PSALM FOR PROTECTION

Psalm 43

A Prayer for Vindication and Deliverance

1   Judge me, O God, and plead my cause
        against an ungodly nation:
        O deliver me from the deceitful and unjust man.

2   For thou *art* the God of my strength:
        why dost thou cast me off?
        Why go I mourning
        because of the oppression of the enemy?

3   O send out thy light and thy truth:
        let them lead me;
        let them bring me unto thy holy hill,
        and to thy tabernacles.

4   Then will I go unto the altar of God,
        unto God my exceeding joy:
        yea, upon the harp will I praise thee,
        O God my God.

5   Why art thou cast down, O my soul?
        And why art thou disquieted within me?
        Hope in God: for I shall yet praise him,
        who is the health of my countenance, and my God.

PSALM FOR VICTORY

Psalm 149
Israel Exhorted to Praise the LORD

1 Praise ye the LORD.
    Sing unto the LORD a new song,
    and his praise in the congregation of saints.
2 Let Israel rejoice in him that made him:
    let the children of Zion be joyful in their King.
3 Let them praise his name in the dance:
    let them sing praises unto him with the timbrel and harp.
4 For the LORD taketh pleasure in his people:
    he will beautify the meek with salvation.
5 Let the saints be joyful in glory:
    let them sing aloud upon their beds.
6 *Let* the high *praises* of God *be* in their mouth,
    and a two-edged sword in their hand;
7 to execute vengeance upon the heathen,
    and punishments upon the people;
8 to bind their kings with chains,
    and their nobles with fetters of iron;
9 to execute upon them the judgment written:
    this honor have all his saints.
    Praise ye the LORD.

PSALM AGAINST PERSECUTION

Psalm 142
A Prayer for Help in Trouble
Maschil of David; A prayer when he was in the cave

1   I cried unto the LORD with my voice;
      with my voice unto the LORD did I make my supplication.
2   I poured out my complaint before him;
      I showed before him my trouble.
3   When my spirit was overwhelmed within me,
      then thou knewest my path.
      In the way wherein I walked
      have they privily laid a snare for me.
4   I looked on *my* right hand, and beheld,
      but *there was* no man that would know me:
      refuge failed me;
      no man cared for my soul.
5   I cried unto thee, O LORD:
      I said, Thou *art* my refuge
      and my portion in the land of the living.
6   Attend unto my cry;
      for I am brought very low:
      deliver me from my persecutors;
      for they are stronger than I.

7   Bring my soul out of prison,
         that I may praise thy name:
         the righteous shall compass me about;
         for thou shalt deal bountifully with me.

PSALM OF THANKSGIVING

Psalm 137
The Mourning of the Exiles in Babylon

1   By the rivers of Babylon,
        there we sat down, yea, we wept,
        when we remembered Zion.

2   We hanged our harps upon the willows in the midst thereof.

3   For there they that carried us away captive required of us a song;
        and they that wasted us *required of us* mirth, *saying,*
        Sing us *one* of the songs of Zion.

4   How shall we sing the LORD's song in a strange land?

5   If I forget thee, O Jerusalem,
        let my right hand forget *her cunning.*

6   If I do not remember thee,
        let my tongue cleave to the roof of my mouth;
        if I prefer not Jerusalem above my chief joy.

7   Remember, O LORD, the children of Edom
        in the day of Jerusalem;
        who said, Rase *it,* rase *it,*
        even to the foundation thereof.

8   O daughter of Babylon, who art to be destroyed;
        happy *shall he be,* that rewardeth thee as thou hast served us. (Rev. 18.6)

9   Happy *shall he be,* that taketh and dasheth
        thy little ones against the stones.

PSALM FOR HEALING

Psalm 23
The LORD Is My Shepherd
A Psalm of David

1   The LORD *is* my shepherd; I shall not want.
2   He maketh me to lie down in green pastures:
      he leadeth me beside the still waters. (Rev. 7:17)
3   He restoreth my soul:
      he leadeth me in the paths of righteousness for his name's
      sake.
4   Yea, though I walk through the valley of the shadow of death,
      I will fear no evil: for thou *art* with me;
      thy rod and thy staff they comfort me.
5   Thou preparest a table before me in the presence of mine
      enemies:
      thou anointest my head with oil;
      my cup runneth over.
6   Surely goodness and mercy shall follow me all the days of
      my life:
      and I will dwell in the house of the LORD for ever.

PSALM FOR GUIDANCE

Psalm 25
A Prayer for Guidance, Pardon, and Protection
A Psalm of David

1   Unto thee, O LORD, do I lift up my soul.
2   O my God, I trust in thee:
      let me not be ashamed,
      let not mine enemies triumph over me.
3   Yea, let none that wait on thee be ashamed:
      let them be ashamed which transgress without cause.
4   Show me thy ways, O LORD;
      teach me thy paths.
5   Lead me in thy truth, and teach me:
      for thou *art* the God of my salvation;
      on thee do I wait all the day.
6   Remember, O LORD, thy tender mercies and thy loving-kindnesses;
      for they *have been* ever of old.
7   Remember not the sins of my youth, nor my transgressions:
      according to thy mercy remember thou me
      for thy goodness' sake, O LORD.
8   Good and upright *is* the LORD:
      therefore will he teach sinners in the way.
9   The meek will he guide in judgment:
      and the meek will he teach his way.

10 All the paths of the LORD *are* mercy and truth
　　　　unto such as keep his covenant and his testimonies.
11 For thy name's sake, O LORD,
　　　　pardon mine iniquity; for it *is* great.
12 What man *is* he that feareth the LORD?
　　　　Him shall he teach in the way *that* he shall choose.
13 His soul shall dwell at ease;
　　　　and his seed shall inherit the earth.
14 The secret of the LORD *is* with them that fear him;
　　　　and he will show them his covenant.
15 Mine eyes *are* ever toward the LORD;
　　　　for he shall pluck my feet out of the net.
16 Turn thee unto me, and have mercy upon me;
　　　　for I *am* desolate and afflicted.
17 The troubles of my heart are enlarged:
　　　　O bring thou me out of my distresses.
18 Look upon mine affliction and my pain;
　　　　and forgive all my sins.
19 Consider mine enemies; for they are many;
　　　　and they hate me with cruel hatred.
20 O keep my soul, and deliver me:
　　　　let me not be ashamed; for I put my trust in thee.
21 Let integrity and uprightness preserve me;
　　　　for I wait on thee.
22 Redeem Israel, O God,
　　　　out of all his troubles.

PSALM OF PRAISE

Psalm 113
Praise for Exalting the Humble

1   Praise ye the LORD.
      Praise, O ye servants of the LORD,
      praise the name of the LORD.
2   Blessed be the name of the LORD
      from this time forth and for evermore.
3   From the rising of the sun
      unto the going down of the same
      the LORD's name *is* to be praised.
4   The LORD *is* high above all nations,
      and his glory above the heavens.
5   Who *is* like unto the LORD our God,
      who dwelleth on high,
6   who humbleth *himself* to behold
      the things that are in heaven, and in the earth!
7   He raiseth up the poor out of the dust,
      and lifteth the needy out of the dunghill;
8   that he may set *him* with princes,
      even with the princes of his people.
9   He maketh the barren woman to keep house,
      and to be a joyful mother of children.
      Praise ye the LORD.

PSALM FOR DELIVERANCE

Psalm 6

A Prayer for Mercy in Time of Trouble

To the chief Musician on Neg'inoth upon
Shem'inith, A Psalm of David

1 O LORD, rebuke me not in thine anger,
    neither chasten me in thy hot displeasure. (Ps. 38.1)

2 Have mercy upon me, O LORD; for I *am* weak:
    O LORD, heal me; for my bones are vexed.

3 My soul is also sore vexed:
    but thou, O LORD, how long?

4 Return, O LORD, deliver my soul:
    oh save me for thy mercies' sake.

5 For in death *there is* no remembrance of thee:
    in the grave who shall give thee thanks?

6 I am weary with my groaning;
    all the night make I my bed to swim;
    I water my couch with my tears.

7 Mine eye is consumed because of grief;
    it waxeth old because of all mine enemies.

8 Depart from me, all ye workers of iniquity; (Mt. 7:23) · (Luke 13:27)
    for the LORD hath heard the voice of my weeping.

9 The LORD hath heard my supplication;
    the LORD will receive my prayer.

10 Let all mine enemies be ashamed and sore vexed:
    let them return *and* be ashamed suddenly.

17 Deal bountifully with thy servant,
    that I may live, and keep thy word.
18 Open thou mine eyes,
    that I may behold wondrous things out of thy law.
19 I *am* a stranger in the earth:
    hide not thy commandments from me.
20 My soul breaketh for the longing
    that it hath unto thy judgments at all times.
              Ps. 119:17–20

Thy hands have made me and fashioned me: give me understanding, that I may learn thy commandments.

                         Ps. 119:73

Do you want to give me your life?
Do you want to give me your heart?

Do you want to give me your life?
Sinner, I have died for you.

PART VI

Therefore I say unto you, Take no thought for your life, what ye shall eat, or what ye shall drink; nor yet for your body, what ye shall put on. Is not the life more than meat, and the body than raiment?

26: Behold the fowls of the air: for they sow not, neither do they reap, nor gather into barns; yet your heavenly Father feedeth them. Are ye not much better than they?

27: Which of you by taking thought can add one cubit unto his stature?

28: And why take ye thought for raiment? Consider the lilies of the field, how they grow; they toil not, neither do they spin:

29: And yet I say unto you, That even Solomon in all his glory was not arrayed like one of these.

30: Wherefore, if God so clothe the grass of the field, which to day is, and to morrow is cast into the oven, shall he not much more clothe you, O ye of little faith?

GOOD MORNING, LORD

I am ready to start a new day.
Keep me strong in your Word.
Here I am bowing very low before you
Do not let bad words coming out of my mouth
Give me strength to always work
in all the corners of the land.

Good morning, Lord

I come before you once more
To tell you that I had slept well
Even though everything was not normal
Please help me.
I feel that I am no longer in the world
Because all the calamities
And all the problems come at once.
Help me to stay calm in order for all to disappear
Before the day is over.
Help me to forget all those problems
So I can concentrate on you more.

WHAT TO SAY ABOUT LIFE?

Everyday life experiences changes;
However one does not live better days.
The existence, in fact is robbed of happiness.
Suffering is very bad, but one suffers often.

In this bitter life, everything seems scary,
One cannot talk to us about life, happiness.
One cannot feel well when facing woes
Unless one acts as though he does not see his troubles.

Life is like a hot wire on which one sits for deliverance.
Only the deliverance can take someone away from their sentence.

MELENE SAINT ANGE "LELENE"

PRECIOUS THOUGHTS

THE REVELATION OF GOD

The spiritual life of a Christian is not an option. The relation with God is the very foundation of the progression in the Christian life.

OUR PRAYER

The LORD bless thee, and keep thee:
25: The LORD make his face shine upon thee, and be gracious unto thee:
26: The LORD lift up his countenance upon thee, and give thee peace.

Num. 6:24–26

I WAS ASTRAY WITHOUT GOD

I only had as friends people who were interested in mundane pleasure. All seemed to to be rosy. But I was playing with fire without realizing it for I was as a crazy woman for the things of the world. Music, theater, dance, cinema, balls, indecent clothing were my priorities. But God in his infinite compassion has come down in the very bottom of the pit to save me, and to make of me a regenerated woman thanks to his purifying blood.

2 Cor. 5:17

If any man be in Christ, He is a new creature. The old things have passed away, and behold everything has become new.

PRECIOUS THOUGHTS

The Testimony

The Christian testimony must always be founded on what one has actually lived. Not one soul will be impressed by a witness of Christianity which limits themselves saying, "I have perceived a great tumult, but I did not know what it was."

TESTIMONY

I was born and raised in a Christian home. After the death of my mother, I had tears in my eyes that could not dry. But discouragement for me was a violent passion. Life became tasteless. Nothing was beautiful to me. I was seeking refuge, so that grief would not break my heart completely.

I went to several churches asking for help with prayer request; I could never find any. But I got so discouraged. I started noticing that everyone was minding his/her own business. Then I threw myself in the world: pleasure from left to right. You would find me in all balls, carnivals. I would not miss one program.

I thought I had made it so much that I formed a group which started to travel all over in all corners of the country (Haiti), and I even forgot where I had come from. Once after I finished partying in my native town, Hinche (Haiti), in December 2000, the driver lost control of the brake in a place called Monn Kabrit. It overturned, but God saved me because he had a plan for me.

One day I started meditating, and I felt guilty. Then I started thinking and I felt there is a work that I could do, but that had never come to my mind. When I thought of the event of September 11, I could have been one the people who had died, but my life had not been ready for paradise. This is the greatest lesson I learned. And I will always tell someone who does not place their trust in the Lord that they are missing out a lot.

I left the world; I gave my back to it because I did not get anything out of it. Now I have returned to my place. Everything that I used to do in the world I will not do it anymore. When Satan saw that, he got angry because he realized that I turned my back to him.

After two years, my house got burned. I did not know what to do, but God helped me come out of that trouble.

Friend, friend, when God needs you, there is no place where you can be that he would not take you. He took me and he told me, "I know that you are seeking a refuge, a friend to talk to in need. Well, come to me for help." That is the reason why I have written this book titled:

IN THE BIBLE

In the Bible you will find exactly everything you need: answer to the questions of life.

No man can serve two masters: for either he will hate the one, and love the other; or else he will hold to the one, and despise the other. Ye cannot serve God and mammon.

Matt. 6:24

PERFECTION

Each person will have a strong struggle to go through in order to triumph over sin in one's own heart. Sometimes it is discouraging because we see the fault of our character, and we stop to consider them whereas it would be better to look at Jesus and put on his robe of righteousness.

JESUS WILL NEVER CHANGE

Jesus healed someone who had leprosy.
Jesus calmed a great wind.
Jesus healed two people who had evil spirit.
Jesus healed someone who was paralyzed.
Jesus healed two blind people.
Jesus healed someone who was deaf.
Jesus did great miracles for you and for me.

Do not forget the same Jesus who was there yesterday, is there today, and forever.

PRECIOUS THOUGHTS

For God so loved the world, that he gave his only begotten Son, that whosoever believeth in him should not perish, but have everlasting life.

JESUS'S TEACHING ON FASTING

16 ¶ Moreover when ye fast, be not, as the hypocrites, of a sad countenance: for they disfigure their faces, that they may appear unto men to fast. Verily I say unto you, They have their reward.

17 But thou, when thou fastest, anoint thine head, and wash thy face;

18 that thou appear not unto men to fast, but unto thy Father which is in secret: and thy Father which seeth in secret shall reward thee openly.

STOP STOP

Stop hurting your neighbor
Stop betraying your neighbor
Stop killing with your tongue
Stop making the church suffer
Stop being busybodies
Stop believing that you are the owner of the church
Stop sending people to hell
Stop making people cry
Stop causing people to leave the church
Stop passing the bulk
Stop troubling people's sleep
Stop! Stop! Stop!
because Jesus is coming.
Get converted! Get converted! Get converted!
so that you can have life forever.
Stop!

Experience was yesterday. Let us answer the problems of today.

Always support your neighbor.

VICTORY

In the conflict where we are engaged as Christians, we must be active in the combat of faith and passive in the struggle against sin.

What the Christian must have: faith
1) Faith heals.
2) Faith strengthens.
3) Faith relieves.
4) Faith calms the heart.
5) Faith brings happiness.
6) Faith brings courage.
7) Faith warms up the heart.
8) Faith is a source of life.
9) Faith brings happiness.
10) Faith fights evil thoughts.
11) Faith makes noble.
12) Faith transforms situations.

NEVER ALONE

Jesus can calm water
Even when you are walking in darkness
Do not get discouraged
Know that the Lord is there
He will never forsake you
He will never leave you alone
What a good friend Jesus is!

He is there in both bad times and good times.
He is always there
even when you live day after day
know that there is a father
who is with you forever.

THE TRUE ENEMY OF THE CHRISTIAN: DOUBT

Introduction

Very often some people think that our true enemies are our neighbors that are envious of the fact that we are progressing. Others think that our colleagues at work hate us because of a promotion. According to the Bible or on a spiritual point of view, the true enemy of a Christian is doubt.

The Effect of Doubt or the Consequences of Doubt:

1) Doubt paralyzes the body.
2) Doubt causes heart palpitation.
3) Doubt provokes the lack of confidence.
4) Doubt handicaps the person.
5) Doubt makes life bitter.
6) Doubt brings trouble.
7) Doubt breaks friendship.
8) Doubt stays on the way of happiness.
9) Doubt is the enemy of progress.
10) Doubt makes the person stupid.
11) Doubt dries up the bones.
12) Doubt brings sadness.
13) Doubt betrays good mood.
14) Doubt makes the person foolish.

PRAYER

Lord, make of me a worker of your peace.
Lord, make of me a builder of your love.
Where there is hatred, let me bring love.

Let me console rather than being consoled.
Let me understand rather than being understood.

For one must know how to give to be showered;
For one must forget self to find oneself . . .

St. Francis of Assisi

Eph. 5:20

Giving thanks always for all things unto God and the Father in the
name of our Lord Jesus Christ;

Col. 3.16, 17

Behold, I stand at the door, and knock: if any man hear my voice,
and open the door, I will come in to him, and will sup with him,
and he with me.

God's Calling

Repeat with me

Thank you, Lord for this love calling.

I, poor sinner, I desire fervently serving you for the rest of my life.

If you have repeated this prayer with me, call me at the following number:

(561) 502-8757

PART VII

PRECIOUS THOUGHTS

Christian

As straight as may be your life, no matter the number of good deeds that you accomplish; as religious as you may appear to be, you are not a true Christian if you do not know Jesus Christ personally and intimately. Acting good will never make you a Christian, but just a person of good morality.

A Christian does what is righteous because s/he is a Christian, never to become a Christian.

Sin

The problem of sin, being more profound than a bad conduct, and our nature being sinful from the moment of birth in this world of sin, the answer to the problem of sin must be researched outside of the behavior or conduct. God proposes to start anew.

Faith

Faith persists in trusting God even in adverse circumstances. It is easy to trust in him when everything is smooth in life. But when it seems that our prayers remain unanswered, faith is truly put to the test. The Lord desires that you put your trust in his love and in his mercy in the midst of clouds and darkness as well as under the sun rays.

Positive thoughts do not produce true faith, but faith produces positive thoughts.

Surrender

The only conscious effort to pursue during a Christian life consists of seeking God. It will result in an instinctive effort to reach other goals.

During their spiritual growth, Christians surrender to the Lord from time to time. At some point they give themselves to God, and other times they trust in themselves.

Temptation

Regarding temptation, the true question to know is whether or not we live our lives independently of Christ.

www.ingramcontent.com/pod-product-compliance
Lightning Source LLC
Chambersburg PA
CBHW031219120626
46545CB00003B/916